HAIKU
AND
HICCUPS

Dimitri Gonis

Till & Washington Publishing

First published by Till & Washington 2023
tillandwashington@hotmail.com

Copyright © 2023 Dimitri Gonis

ISBN: 978-0-645735-11-6

This is a work of fiction. Any similarities between places and characters are a coincidence.

Cover image: Dimitri Gonis

Images copyright © Dimitri Gonis
Image 30 (starry night) by Christos Gonis

Layout and typesetting: Busybird Publishing

Busybird Publishing
2/118 Para Road
Montmorency, Victoria
Australia 3094

www.busybird.com.au

About the Author

Dimitri Gonis was born in Melbourne, Australia. When he was twelve, his family repatriated to Greece where they lived in a small village outside Pylos in the southern Peloponnese. He credits this period of his life with inspiring his writing. After finishing his secondary education in Greece, he returned to Melbourne where he completed his tertiary studies. He currently lectures in the Department of Languages and Linguistics at La Trobe University Melbourne, Australia. His opinion pieces have been published in Australia and abroad.

Haiku and Hiccups is his first collection of poems.

To Yianni

CONTENTS

Prologue

A teardrop said to a raindrop
'I envy the heights from which you fall'

'And I the depths from which you rise'
It replied

In the bud of a rose
Deep within its folds
Fields of wheat and siestas celebrate life

Darkened, lonely trunks
Giants poisoned for the light
Scattered in a field

A sunset's fading glow
Is a reminder
To love and apologise

A petal trembles
Cicadas prepare to trill
Chestnuts explode

A brown boy is smiling
His feet never touch the earth
His black bike is his carpet

Distant, elusive lights

Vain dreams and promises

Are an inverted illusion that mocks us when we smile

Gnarled hands
Whose birthday was only yesterday
Stroke the knotted prickly pear

Transient flickers
Supernovas in the dark
That leave empty chairs

Forlorn is the view
From the jagged crest of time
The abyss endless

Matches on a ledge
Untouched by wind and rain
Lit up dreams again

Blue skies, blue eyes
Her room is her cocoon
Too small for her smile

In the waning dusk
Even our worst memories
Soften our sad fall

With fireflies we dance
Around pyres of our hopes
Smitten, bitten, duped

Snowflakes on a bough
Captured shadows of the night
In a kaleidoscope of sighs

In a drop of dew
Summers and winters caress
Old men reminisce

Once there was singing
Amongst the barley and reeds
But it has all gone

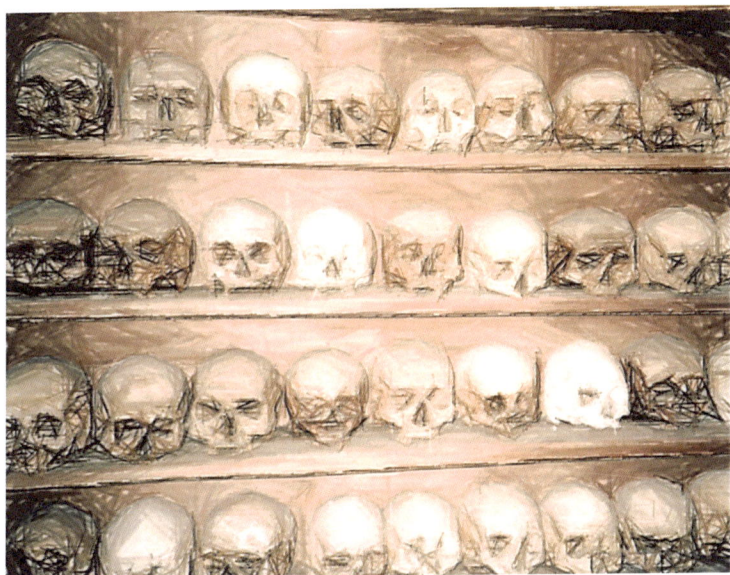

Silently it slides
Closer and closer it comes
To ridicule our innocence

A breeze blows gently
Leaves shimmer in the moonlight
Of a yard's extinguished dreams

The pyrotechnics of youth
Fizzled out too soon
There was no time to make a wish

An eagle was killed for pleasure
Its mate cried out all day
Then they killed it too

Close your eyes and ears
Thick mist blankets the mountains
Grapevines kiss the sun

In an old man's stoop
A shy boy serenades the moon
A grey horse prances
A tiny bell is always jingling

Musty scents of age
In the wadding of a toy
Locked up in a trunk

It is night, dark night
No one there to watch the dance
Of branches and light

She spoke to her walls
Summer, Winter, Autumn, Spring
Until they replied

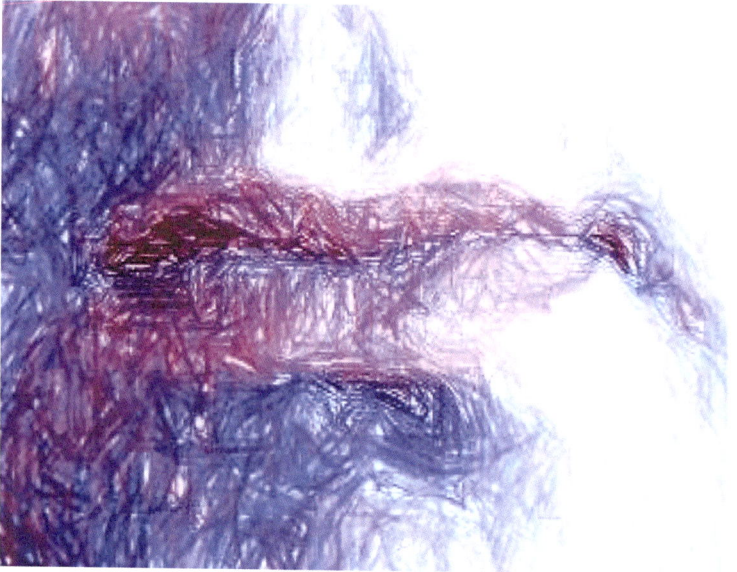

Angry lips crushed
The sunlight
Once eagerly suspended over smiles

Numbers were once the measure of height
Now balmy nights with cricket choirs
Are all that really matters

A willow wept and wept
In the end it slowly died
After Callistemon called

A dream was tucked away
Inside a birch tree's hollow
But someone burnt the tree

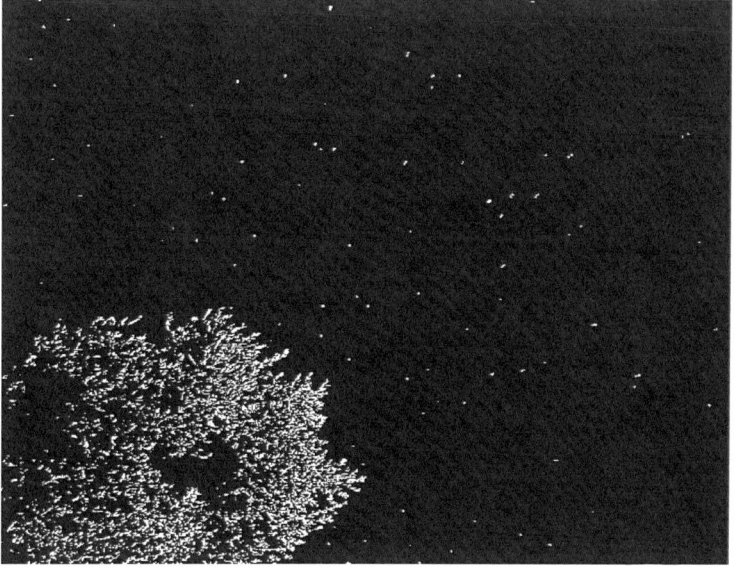

Stars glitter and fall
Above fleeting scribbles of stories
Penned in a hurry

Swallows never came
They heard about the pain
From the bougainvillea

The universe speaks to us
It whispers its secrets through the breeze
And in the rustle of the leaves

For fear of the night
We all clamour round the light
Only to be stung

An old streetlight pries
Through the shutters of a house
With great acoustics

When the rains arrived
With thunderclaps and lightning
We all huddled around our fires

The shadow has gone
Along with the contours and colours
That once formed it

Raindrops pitter patter
On the canvas in the yard
To distant melodies and echoes of lost love

Nostalgia is like a place
Where rats nibble on dreams
Abandoned to the silence

Two majestic snails
Abducted from the seabed
Were boiled for their shells

The balcony is bare
No chairs or conversations
Only citrus trees below

When two beetles kiss
Sparkling eyes are filled with awe
Velvet souls flutter

Epilogue

Somewhere
A sun is clearing a peak
Rays of light pierce
Mist-cloaked trees in cemeteries

www.ingramcontent.com/pod-product-compliance
Lightning Source LLC
Chambersburg PA
CBRC100735150426
42811CB00065B/1891